Helping Children See Jesus

ISBN: 978-1-64104-032-7

God Is Sovereign

Old Testament Volume 27:
Ezra, Nehemiah

Author: Arlene S. Piepgrass
Illustrator: Vernon Henkel
Typesetting and Layout: Patricia Pope

© 2019 Bible Visuals International
PO Box 153, Akron, PA 17501-0153
Phone: (717) 859-1131
www.biblevisuals.org

RELATED ITEMS

To access related items (such as activities, memory verse posters and translated texts) please visit our web store at shop.biblevisuals.org and enter 2027 in the search box on the page.

FREE TEXT DOWNLOAD

To access a FREE printable copy of the teaching text (PDF format) in English or other available languages, enter S2027DL in the search box. Add the item to your cart, and use coupon code XTACSV17 at checkout. Once your order is processed you will receive an email with a link to the free download.

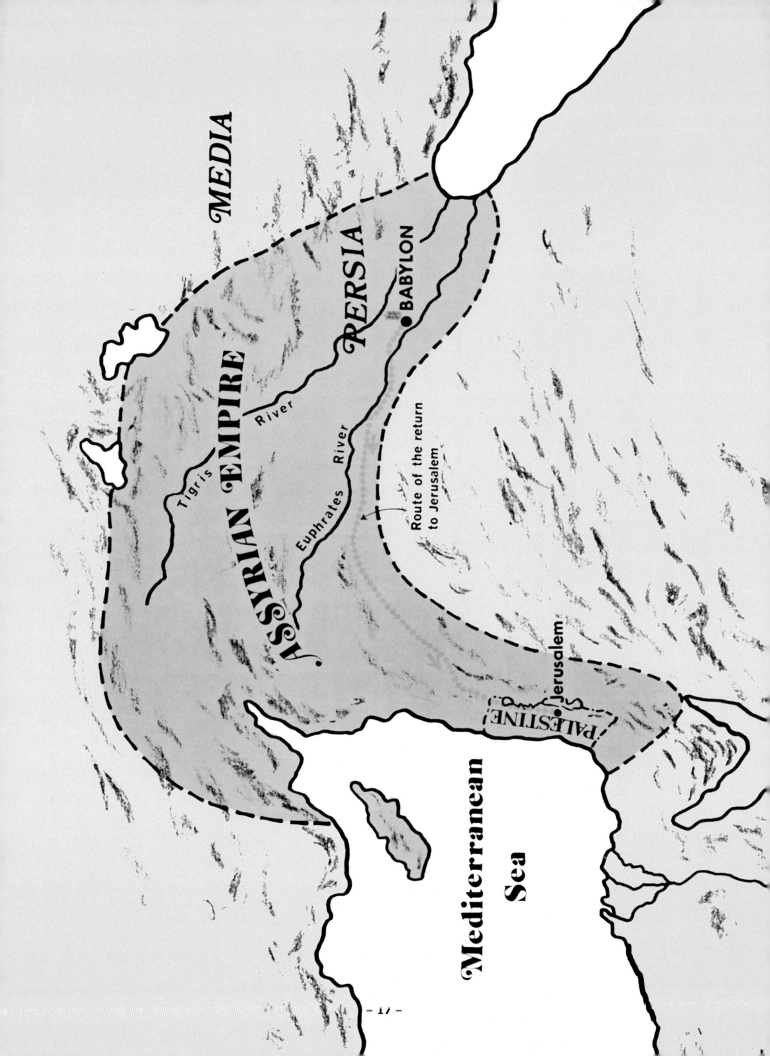

MEDIA

PERSIA

ASSYRIAN EMPIRE

Tigris River

Euphrates River

● BABYLON

Route of the return
to Jerusalem

PALESTINE

● Jerusalem

Mediterranean
Sea

The hand of our God is upon all them for good that seek Him; but His power and His wrath is against all them that forsake Him.

Ezra 8:22b

-18-

NOTE TO THE TEACHER

The captivity of Israel is related in the final lesson of Kings and Chronicles. (See Old Testament Volume 26.) If you have not taught that material recently, give your students the following brief background.

Israel was God's special nation. (See Deuteronomy 7:6.) In His sovereignty, God had three purposes for the Israelite people. They were to be (1) His witnesses to heathen nations; (2) The channels through whom He would give His written Word and (3) The nation through which He would send His Son, the Lord Christ Jesus. Christ would be the Saviour of the world.

God promised (through Moses) to bless the Israelites if they obeyed Him. (See Deuteronomy 6:24-25.) He also warned of punishment if they disobeyed (Deuteronomy 28:36-37). Years later, King Solomon built a beautiful temple in Jerusalem. And the Lord God repeated His promise and warning (1 Kings 9:3-9).

Israel ignored God's commandments. The Israelite kings sinned greatly against the Lord. The people followed the sinful ways of their kings. God sent prophets to warn the Israelites. But they despised God's words and laughed at His messengers. The Lord was true to what He had said. His people, the Israelites, were punished. They were taken as captives to Assyria (2 Kings 17:4-6) and to Babylon (2 Kings 24:12-14; 25:7-12). Their Babylonian captors were later conquered and ruled by Persia.

God's people were in captivity 70 years. But the Lord did not forget them. The sovereign Lord had a plan for them. Through His prophets, God reminded Israel of the reasons for their captivity. (See Jeremiah 25:1-11.) He also promised they would return to Palestine after 70 years. (See Jeremiah 29:10-14.)

The book of Ezra opens after the 70 years of captivity. God sovereignly used heathen kings to fulfill His plan for Israel.

Teacher: Print boldly on a large poster:

GOD IS SOVEREIGN
God rules His entire creation

Display poster during each lesson. Repeatedly emphasize that God is sovereign–the *only* Sovereign.

Scripture to be studied: Ezra 1:1–6:22; Haggai 1:1–2:23; Zechariah 1:3-4; 16-17

The *aim* of the lesson: To show that God controlled the affairs of the Israelite nation.

What your students should *know*: That God fulfills His warnings as well as His promises.

What your students should *feel*: Confidence in God as they obey Him.

What your students should *do*: Trust God to work out His plan in their lives.

Lesson outline (for the teacher's and students' notebooks):

1. God remembers His promise (Ezra 1:1-11).
2. God strengthens the leaders (Ezra 3:1-13).
3. God knows the opposition (Ezra 4:1-5:17).
4. God intervenes for His people (Ezra 6:1-22; Haggai 1:1–2:23; Zecharriah 1:3-4; 16-17).

The verse to be memorized:

The hand of our God is upon all them for good that seek Him; but His power and His wrath is against all them that forsake Him. (Ezra 8:22b)

THE LESSON

Sovereign is a word some may not hear often. Perhaps you never have heard it. It tells us something special about God. Sovereign means that God is in absolute control of everything everywhere. He rules the entire universe. (Show poster.)

Today we begin studying the Bible books of Ezra and Nehemiah and the prophets, **HAGGAI, ZECHARIAH** and **MALACHI**. Was God sovereign over the heathen kings of long ago? Could He accomplish His purpose for the people of Israel whom He chose for Himself? Listen carefully!

1. GOD REMEMBERS HIS PROMISE
Ezra 1:1-11

The sun rose in a small Persian village. Women went to the village well for water. Young men worked in their gardens. Children played in the courtyards. So it was each day in that far-away land 2500 years ago. (*Teacher:* Show back cover map. Point out location of Persia in relation to Palestine.)

Not all who lived in Persia were Persians. Many were Jews. Do you wonder why Jews were living in Persia? Let us imagine some old Jewish men talking about the past.

Show Illustration #1

"How I wish I were home in Jerusalem," Grandfather Elam said. "Remember our beautiful temple there?" (Point to temple on illustration #1.)

"I wonder if I shall ever see it again," Joel mused longingly.

"If only we had obeyed the laws of God," Harim said sorrowfully. "God commanded us to worship only Him. He said we were NOT to make gold and silver idols. (Point to idol on illustration.) He told us over and over not to worship such gods. He warned us that if we did so, enemy nations would conquer us. He said they would take us to their lands as captives." (Indicate chained arms on illustration #1.)

"We refused to listen to the Lord God," Joel added. "Remember how some of our people sinfully married into heathen families? The heathen do not believe in the true and living God. God had told us never to marry the heathen. But we disobeyed Him." (See Ezra 5:12.)

"We acted as if God did not mean what He said. We were wrong!" Elam added solemnly. "I shall never forget that dreadful day the Babylonians captured us. Remember the humiliation of marching to their land? Since then, the Persians have captured the Babylonians–and us! If only we had obeyed God. Now we are suffering the punishment we deserve. God warned us over and over again. But we chose our own way."

"Remember how we used to sing back home in Palestine? Here, we never sing," said Joel. (See Psalm 137:1-6.) "Do you think we shall ever see Jerusalem again?"

"Yes, I think we shall," said Harim. "Remember what God's prophet, Jeremiah, said? 'For thus saith the LORD, that after 70 years be accomplished at Babylon I will visit you, and perform my good word toward you, in causing you to return to this place. For I know the thoughts that I think toward you, saith the Lord, thoughts of peace, and not of evil, to give you an expected end.' (Jeremiah 29:10-11.) We now have been here 70 years. I believe the Lord will keep His promise. Perhaps soon He will lead us to our homeland."

Just then Harim's grandson came running. "Grandfather!" he shouted. "The king's messenger has come on his horse. He says everyone is to meet together. He will read a proclamation from King Cyrus. Come, Grandfather! Everyone must listen."

The villagers gathered quickly. *Will this be good or bad news*? they wondered.

The messenger unrolled his parchment scroll. "Hear ye! Hear the proclamation of Cyrus, king of Persia! 'Thus says Cyrus, king of Persia, the LORD God of Heaven has given me all the kingdoms of the earth. He has appointed me to build a house (temple) at Jerusalem . . . Whoever there is among you of all His people . . . let him go up to Jerusalem . . . and rebuild the house of the LORD God of Israel. . . And whoever remains in any place where he lives, let that person give silver, gold, goods, cattle, and freewill offerings for the house of God which is in Jerusalem'." (See Ezra 1:2-4.)

Imagine that! Cyrus, the heathen king of Persia, was releasing God's people. He was sending them back to Jerusalem. And he commanded them to rebuild their temple.

Nearly 200 years earlier, God had foretold that Cyrus would release the Jews. Cyrus was not even born when God said this. (See Isaiah 44:28, 45:1.) Cyrus was a heathen king who did not know God (Isaiah 45:7). Yet the Lord caused King Cyrus to accomplish His purpose. The Lord God rules over everyone everywhere. He is sovereign–the only Sovereign.

What do you think the Israelites did when they heard the king's message? (Encourage student response.) Immediately many made plans to return to Jerusalem.

2. GOD STRENGTHENS THE LEADERS
Ezra 3:1-13

Surprisingly, not every Jewish family packed to return to their homeland. Many decided to remain in Persia. They enjoyed their homes–and their work–in Persia. Others remembered little about Jerusalem. Seventy years before, they were young. What had the king told those who would remain in Babylon? (Read Ezra 1:4 again.) They were to give gifts of silver, gold, goods, cattle, offerings. These would help pay the expenses of those who went. Their gifts would also help to rebuild God's house in Jerusalem.

(*Teacher:* Read Ezra 1:5.) Who decided to return to Jerusalem? (*The ones whose hearts God stirred up*) What does this tell us about the sovereignty of God? (*He is the One Who causes people to serve Him.*)

Show Illustration #2

At last the day of departure came. Almost 50,000 people were ready to begin the journey. A man named Zerubbabel was their leader. He was related to the royal family in Israel. (See 1 Chronicles 3:17, 19.)

The strong carried their belongings on their backs. Along with the people were mules, horses, and camels.

King Cyrus sent along a huge load of special gifts. He announced: "King Nebuchadnezzar captured your land 70 years ago. He brought from your temple the articles of gold and silver. Now, Zerubbabel, I want you to take back these valuable treasures. You can use these when your temple is rebuilt." Altogether,Cyrus gave the Jews 5,400 gold and silver articles. (See Ezra 1:11.) What an encouragement that was for the Jewish people!

So the caravan began the long journey back to Palestine. Day after day, week after week, month after month they walked. How long the journey was! How tired they became! On and on they trudged for about 900 miles. (*Teacher:* Compare to a distance familiar to students.)

At last they reached their beloved city. "Jerusalem is in ruins!" Elam cried.

Joel wailed, "Our beautiful temple is only a pile of rubble! Maybe we should have stayed in Persia."

Harim spoke up. "Friends, let us thank God for sending us home. Many young men are with us. We shall rebuild our city and our temple!"

And that is exactly what Zerubbabel led them to do.

First the Israelites settled in nearby towns. Then they all gathered in Jerusalem.

Zerubbabel, Jeshua the priest and their brothers built an altar. They offered sacrifices to God and celebrated the Jewish feast days.

Zerubbabel announced, "It is now time to rebuild our temple. King Cyrus has provided us with all we need. Let us arise and build!"

About seven months later the foundation of the temple was completed. What a day of celebration that was! The priests and Levites played their trumpets and cymbals. The people shouted for joy. They sang, "Praise the Lord for He is good. His loving-kindness is upon Israel forever!"

3. GOD KNOWS THE OPPOSITION
Ezra 4:1-5:17

Not everyone was glad that the Jewish people were back home. A group of Samaritans lived in Palestine during the Jews' captivity. They were not happy that the Jews had returned.

One day some of their leaders made a suggestion to Zerubbabel. "Let us help you build your temple," they said. "We, too, worship a god. We would like to join you."

Show Illustration #3

Zerubbabel shook his head firmly. "No, you cannot help us," he declared. "You do not serve the true and living God. You have idolatry in your worship. You cannot join us. King Cyrus commanded that we Jews build the temple of our God."

What do you think of Zerubbabel's response? (Encourage discussion. Read 2 Corinthians 6:14. Remind students that God warns against linking our lives with unbelievers.)

The Samaritans were insulted and angry. "Those Jews will not let us help them build their temple! We shall make them sorry for their decision," they threatened.

So the Samaritans sent a letter to the king of Persia. Cyrus had died and a new king was on the throne. The Samaritans wrote: "The Jews will rebel against you after they rebuild

Jerusalem. They will refuse to pay their taxes. We warn you, O king, the Jews are dangerous people."

Was this true? No! Indeed, the letter was filled with lies. But the new king believed the lies. He sent a message to the Samaritans.

When the Samaritans received the king's message, they were delighted. They hurried to Jerusalem. Quickly they found Zerubbabel. "Listen to this letter from the king of Persia," they said. "'Command these men to stop building. This city is not to be built until another commandment shall be given from me'." (See Ezra 4:21-22.)

Sadness settled over the Jewish community. In every house that night there were many questions. "Why has God allowed His work to be hindered? Why is He letting heathen people stop us? Why? Why? Why?"

The work did stop. For about 15 years the temple and the city lay silent. Had God forgotten about the Jews? No. Certainly the God of Heaven knows when men hinder His work.

4. GOD INTERVENES FOR HIS PEOPLE
Ezra 6:1-22; Haggai 1:1-2:23; Zechariah 1:1-17

The people may have forgotten God. But He had never forgot them. He sent to them another prophet, **HAGGAI**. **HAGGAI** spoke only what God told him.

HAGGAI announced, "Listen! I have a message from God. This is what He, the Lord Almighty says: 'You wonder why you never have enough to eat. You wonder why you are poor, even though you work hard. You wonder why there is no rain for your gardens'." (See Haggai 1:6-11.)

"This is what the Lord says," **HAGGAI** continued. "You have built nice houses for yourselves. But you have forgotten about My house–My temple. It is in ruins and you do not care." (See Haggai 1:4.)

Then **HAGGAI** gave to the people this command from God: "Go up to the mountains and gather wood. Use it to rebuild the temple. This will please God and honor Him." (Haggai 1:8.)

HAGGAI had a friend named **ZECHARIAH**. He, too, was a prophet. God gave **ZECHARIAH** this message for the Jews: "Do not be like your fathers who would not listen to God. Return to Him. Obey Him. Then He will bless you." (See Zechariah 1:3, 4, 16, 17.) Then **ZECHARIAH** gave God's people this good news: " God promises that our governor,

Zerubbabel, will finish building the temple! You cannot do it by yourself. But God will help you!" (See Zechariah 4:6.) Oh how this encouraged God's people!

Zerubbabel and all the men obeyed God's command. But again the Samaritans wrote to the king of Persia. Another new king, King Darius, was on the throne. Would he, too, stop the work? (*Teacher:* Read Ezra 5:5.) God caused King Darius to search for the proclamation of King Cyrus. That proclamation, you remember, had been written many years before. The proclamation was exactly as the Jews had reported. Cyrus had indeed commanded the Jews to rebuild their temple.

King Darius wrote to the Samaritans: "Let the Jews be allowed to continue their building." (*Teacher:* Read Ezra 6:6-12.) From then on the builders really worked hard to finish God's house.

Show Illustration #4

Finally, 22 years after the temple had been begun, it was finished. How happy God's people were to dedicate God's house! (See Ezra 6:16.)

The Lord God entrusted to **ZECHA-RIAH** many wonderful prophecies. He told the Jews that their King would come riding on an ass. (See Zechariah 9:9.) He would be sold for 30 pieces of silver. (See Zechariah 11:12.) He would have wounds in His hands. (See Zechariah 13:6.) Think for a moment. Of whom was **ZECHARIAH** prophesying? He was speaking of the Lord Jesus Christ, more than 500 years before Christ was born!

Near the end of his prophecy, **ZECHARIAH** told of a day that is even yet to come. He prophesied, "The LORD shall be King over all the earth. In that day there shall be one LORD." (See Zechariah 14:9.) "And there will be peace in the whole world." (See Zechariah 6:12-13; 12:1-14:21.) In God's time, these prophecies will also come true. It was God who gave the prophecies. And He always keeps His word.

The sovereign God is always the same. He remembers all His promises. He helps all those who honor Him. He knows all about the testings that come to His own. And He makes everything work together for good to those who are His. (See Romans 8:28.) He is sovereign . . . The Lord of Heaven and earth. Have you acknowledged Him as your sovereign? If not, will you do so right now?

Lesson 2
GOD CONVICTS ISRAEL OF SIN

Scripture to be studied: Ezra, chapters 7-10

The *aim* of the lesson: To show that some present consequences of sin are heartache and sorrow.

> **What your students should *know*:** That confession of sin and repentance restore fellowship with God.

> **What your students should *feel*:** A sincere desire to obey God and serve Him.

> **What your students should *do*:** Examine their hearts and confess any hidden sin.

Lesson outline (for the teacher's and students' notebooks):

1. Israel's sin (Ezra 9).
2. Ezra, God's man (Ezra 7 and 8).
3. Ezra's contrite prayer (Ezra 9).
4. Israel's confession and restoration (Ezra 10).

The verse to be memorized:

The hand of our God is upon all them for good that seek Him; but His power and His wrath is against all them that forsake Him. (Ezra 8:22b)

NOTE TO THE TEACHER
Display poster: GOD IS SOVEREIGN. Review the meaning of *sovereign*. Mention the manifestations of God's sovereignty in Lesson #1:

1. God accomplished His plan fo Israel through heathen kings–Cyrus and Darius.
2. God gave 50,000 Israelites the desire to return to Palestine.
3. God protected the Jews who returned to their homeland.

THE LESSON

Listen carefully today for whatever reveals that God is sovereign.

1. ISRAEL'S SIN
Ezra 9

Show Illustration #5

Did you ever throw a pebble into a lake or pool? What happened to the water? (Let students discuss the circle or ripples caused by one pebble.) Sin, like that pebble, may seem trivial. But it is impossible to know the outcome of sin.

Long ago the Jews returned to Jerusalem to rebuild their temple. Why had they been away from their homeland? (*They were captives of the Babylonians and Persians. They were in captivity because they had married heathen. This led them into idol worship. These Jews had ignored God's laws and disobeyed Him.*)

How happy the Jews were to be home in Palestine! Finally, after almost 22 years, their temple was rebuilt. Once again the Israelites could offer sacrifices to God. Many years before the Lord had commanded them (through Moses) to do this. From now on they could celebrate all their religious festivals. Surely they would never again forget God's laws! Or would they?

In Palestine, year after year went by. The older people–including Zerubbabel–died. Boys grew and, in time, became leaders of the people. The new priests led in the sacrifices and temple worship.

Ten years, twenty, thirty years passed. Few talked about life under the Babylonians and Persians. Almost no one remembered how dreadful captivity had been. Forty years went by. They did not discuss *why* God had allowed their capture. No one cared that their people had been Babylonian prisoners.

Could a conversation like this have taken place in a Jewish home?

Ebed, a Jewish youth, spoke to his father. "Ahab has invited me to a party his parents are having. Please may I go?"

"My son, Ahab's parents are Canaanites. They do not worship our God," answered Joab, his father. "They serve false gods and worship idols. They also offer sacrifices to their gods. I do not want you to go to their affairs."

"Oh, please let me go! I promise I shall not worship their idols. They have really good times at their parties. Even our priest is going." (See Ezra 9:1.)

Joab thought a while. With hesitation, he finally replied. "I guess if the priest is going there isn't any harm."

But was there harm in going? (*Yes. God had warned His people against participating in heathen festivities. Indeed, the Jews were to destroy heathen altars and idols. See Exodus 34: 12-16.*)

Months later Ebed again went to his father. "I love Ahab's sister," he said. "I want to marry her. Maybe one day she will worship our God."

Let's see what God had said about that. (Read Ezra 9:12.)

Ebed did marry Ahab's heathen sister. (See Ezra 10:10.) He went to more festivals with her. In time they had children. But Ebed did not teach them about the true God of Heaven.

Ebed had thought that going to a heathen festival was harmless. But it was sin. Why? (*God had forbidden contact with those who did not believe in Him. And one sin led to another.*)

Like Ebed, many Jews married their godless neighbors. They doubtless followed their evil customs. (See Ezra 9:12.) Like the pebble thrown into the water, sin had far-reaching effects. The ripples spread out and touched many lives–even the whole Jewish nation.

2. EZRA, GOD'S MAN
Ezra 7 and 8

King Cyrus had given permission for all Jews to return to Jerusalem. But not all had gone with Zerubbabel. (Review Ezra 1:3-6.) Back in Persia a Jewish boy named Ezra was born. Ezra's father was a priest.

As a boy, Ezra often heard his father speak of God. (See Deuteronomy 6:7.) One day Ezra said, "Father, I want to study God's law. I want to know God's commands so I can obey them. Some day I want to teach His laws to others." (See Ezra 7:10.)

What do you in this class want to do with your life? (Encourage student response. Read Matthew 6:33. Emphasize the wisdom of studying God's Word and teaching it.)

Ezra did not know it, but God had plans for him. One day the Lord gave Ezra a desire to return to Jerusalem. (Read Ezra 7:6, 9.) The sovereign God had chosen Ezra to serve Him.

Ezra could not go to Jerusalem without the king's permission. Earlier, Kings Cyrus and Darius had been friendly to the Jews. But now they were dead. A new king–King Artaxerxes–sat on the throne. Like Cyrus and Darius, Artaxerxes was a heathen king. Would he give Ezra permission to return to Jerusalem?

"Ezra," King Artaxerxes said, "you may return to Jerusalem. Any Jews who want to go with you, may do so. We shall send silver and gold with you. In Jerusalem you can buy animals to sacrifice at your temple. If you need more money, let me know. Our royal treasuries will provide whatever you need."

King Artaxerxes had more to say. "Ezra, in Palestine appoint leaders over your people. Teach everyone the laws of your God. Teach those who know Him and all who do not know Him."

What does this tell us about God? (*He is sovereign over all. He accomplishes His purposes through anyone He chooses.*)

Ezra was delighted. He exclaimed, "Blessed be the LORD God of our fathers, which hath put such a thing as this in the king's heart, to beautify the house of the LORD which is in Jerusalem: and hath extended mercy unto me before the kings, and his counselors, and before all the king's mighty princes" (Ezra 7:27-28a).

Ezra wasted no time preparing for his journey. About 6,000 people joined him–mothers, fathers, children, babies, grandparents.

When the people were ready, Ezra made an announcement. "First we shall fast and pray. Our long journey to Jerusalem will be dangerous. Our children are traveling with us. We are carrying gold and silver for the temple. We are taking everything we own. We have to humble ourselves before God. We must ask the Lord to protect us."

One of the older men had a question. "Ezra, will the king's soldiers go with us for protection?"

"No," Ezra replied. "I told the king that our God protects those who worship Him. (See Ezra 8:22.) I believe this. So I did not ask for a military escort."

Show Illustration #6

When the fast was over, Ezra said, "Let us pray." Silently the people bowed as Ezra led them in prayer.

God was faithful. He did not disappoint Ezra. After traveling four months, everyone arrived safely in Jerusalem (Ezra 7:8-9).

The Lord protected them from robbers all the way (Ezra 8:31).

In Jerusalem Ezra and the leaders weighed the silver and gold. This they took to the temple as King Artaxerxes had commanded. They brought animals to be sacrificed to God in the temple. How grateful they were to be back in their own land! How thankful they were for God's protection while traveling!

3. EZRA'S CONTRITE PRAYER
Ezra 9

Ezra's joy did not last long. One day in Jerusalem a group of Jewish officials came to him. "Our people no longer obey the Lord," the leaders said. "They have married heathen men and women. They no longer come to the temple with sacrifices and offerings. They have no interest in our Jewish religious festivals."

The leaders had more to say. "The Jews are living just like the heathen. Even some of the priests are following heathen practices. They have turned their backs on the Lord God. They no longer teach the people the laws of God."

Ezra was distressed. He tore his clothing. He pulled hair from his head to show his great sadness. Those who shared his grief joined him.

Show Illustration #7

Ezra fell on his knees before the house of God. He lifted his hands to the Lord. "O my God, I am ashamed," he cried. "I am embarrassed even to lift my face to You. Our sins are piled higher than our heads. Our guilt has grown even to the heavens. Through the years our fathers have sinned against You. For that reason we were captured. We were taken to a foreign country as slaves. But You did not forsake us. You caused the kings of Persia to let us return home. You put it in the kings' hearts to help rebuild our temple. O Lord God, what can I say? After all You have done, we have broken Your laws again. You warned us not to marry the heathen. But we have ignored Your warnings. We are guilty. You should punish us. If You destroy all of us, we deserve it."

Gradually a large crowd gathered and cried with Ezra. They realized how greatly they had sinned.

4. ISRAEL'S CONFESSION AND RESTORATION
Ezra 10

Finally a man named Shechaniah spoke to Ezra. "We have sinned. We have disobeyed God. We have married heathen women. We know the Lord is displeased. But we want to make things right. We want to make this covenant with the Lord: We shall give up our heathen wives and their children. We want to obey the Lord God and His commandments."

So Ezra gathered all the men of Israel together. "My fellow Jews," he began, "you have been unfaithful to God. You deserve His punishment. Confess your sin to the Lord God and do His will. Separate yourselves from your heathen wives."

Remember the far-reaching ripples of the pebble tossed in the water? The Jews were feeling the far-reaching ripples of sin. It had not seemed wrong when they became friends with the heathen. They even thought it was all right to marry them. But now, families had to separate. And there was great sorrow.

Show Illustration #8

Good-byes had to be said. Many tears were shed. Innocent children screamed as their heathen mothers grabbed them from their fathers. The consequences of sin are heartache and sorrow.

The Israelites had confessed their sin. Having separated from their heathen families, they were forgiven. Only then could the fierce wrath of God be turned from them. (See Ezra 10:14.)

What kind of person do you want to marry? God gives us a warning about this matter. (*Teacher:* Slowly read 2 Corinthians 6:14a.) God knows what is best for us. A Christian sins when he marries one who has not received the Saviour. And remember: the consequences of sin are heartache and sorrow.

What do we learn about God in this part of His Word?

1. God could have destroyed the Jews for marrying heathen. Instead He sovereignly caused a man (Ezra) to lead them to confess their sin. When they turned from their sin, God forgave them. Once again they worshiped their sovereign Lord.

2. God loved the Israelites. But He hated their sin. God loves you. But He hates your sin. (*Teacher:* Read 1 John 1:9 and Proverbs 28:13. Encourage students to confess each known sin to God. Only then can they enjoy God's forgiveness and freedom from guilt.)

Lesson 3
GOD SENDS NEHEMIAH TO JERUSALEM

NOTE TO THE TEACHER

God is sovereign. That is, He is superior, high above all. God is unequaled; unexcelled. God is always right. God is always in control.

God does whatever He chooses to do, whenever He chooses to do it, for whatever purpose He chooses to do it; and He uses whatever or whomever He chooses.

Why is this so? Because He, Creator and Ruler of all the universe, is sovereign.

This lesson and the next contain teachings from the book of Nehemiah. Again we see that God sovereignly chooses people. He prepares each person to do His work. He plans and controls every detail of life. God is sovereign! Begin the lesson by displaying the poster.

Explain the importance of city walls in Bible days. Those who lived within city walls were protected from their enemies. All their foes always wanted to conquer them.

Scripture to be studied: Nehemiah 1:1-3:32

The *aim* of the lesson: To show that God sovereignly chooses leaders to accomplish His work.

What your students should *know:* That God has the sovereign right to place people where they can serve Him.

What your students should *feel:* Amazed that God has them in the place where they can serve Him.

What your students should *do*: Look for opportunities to serve God this week.

Lesson outline (for the teacher's and students' notebooks):

1. Nehemiah's person (Nehemiah 1:1-3, 11).
2. Nehemiah's prayer (Nehemiah 1:4-11).
3. Nehemiah's plan (Nehemiah 2:1-10).
4. Nehemiah's challenge (Nehemiah 2:11-3:32).

The verse to be memorized:

The hand of our God is upon all them for good that seek Him; but His power and His wrath is against all them that forsake Him. (Ezra 8:22b)

THE LESSON

How many of you chose your own parents? Did you choose the country in which you would be born? Who chose these for you? (*God is sovereign. He chooses and controls everything.*)

It was God who chose your parents. He is the One who planned where you would be born. He even placed you right here for a special purpose. And He has a particular task for you.

1. NEHEMIAH'S PERSON
Nehemiah 1:1-3, 11

Nehemiah was a Jew. He was chosen and prepared by God for a special responsibility. He lived at the same time as Ezra. Who was Ezra? (Review highlights of Lesson 2.)

Ezra had gone to Jerusalem to encourage the Jews there. Hanani, Nehemiah's brother, went along with Ezra. Nehemiah remained in Persia.

Show Illustration #9

God had placed Nehemiah in an important position. Nehemiah was King Artaxerxes' cupbearer. Nehemiah sipped the wine before the king drank it. Thus he guarded the king from poisoning.

Nehemiah was important in the Persian government. But he had concern for his own Jewish people. His parents had taught him the history of the Jews. They taught him about God and God's purpose for Jewish people. (See Nehemiah 1:5-11.)

One day Nehemiah's brother, Hanani, came from Jerusalem to Persia. "Hanani, how are things in Jerusalem?" Nehemiah asked eagerly. "Now that the temple is rebuilt, are the Jews worshiping God? Are they obeying God's commandments? How is Ezra? Is he teaching the people the Word of God?"

Before Hanani could answer, Nehemiah continued, "Are the walls and gates of Jerusalem rebuilt? Is the city beautiful once again?" (***Teacher:*** Explain that ancient cities were surrounded by strong walls. These walls protected the residents from their enemies.)

Nehemiah had many questions. It had been 12 years since Hanani went to Jerusalem with Ezra. Every day Nehemiah had thought about them and prayed for them.

Hanani began, "My brother, the temple has been rebuilt. Once again the priests offer sacrifices to God. Ezra teaches the Word of God. But," Hanani added sadly, "the people are discouraged. They have lost interest in obeying God. Again they mingle with the heathen people living around them. The walls of Jerusalem have not been rebuilt. The gates which were burned are a disgrace. Our city is not protected. No one seems to care. No one is interested in rebuilding the walls."

2. NEHEMIAH'S PRAYER
Nehemiah 1:4-11

Nehemiah loved his Jewish people. He loved God. He wanted God's work to be accomplished. How do you think he felt when he heard Hanani's report? (Let students respond.)

Nehemiah was so sad that he, a grown man, cried. For several days he did not eat. He continually wept and prayed. Oh, how he prayed!

Show Illustration #10

Nehemiah cried, "O God! You are great and awesome. You always keep Your promises. You are loving and kind to those who obey You. O Lord, hear my prayer. I am praying day and night for my Jewish people. I confess that we have disobeyed Your commandments. (Point to tablets of stone on illustration #10.) We have sinned against You. You said if we confess our sins (point to sinful heart), You will forgive us. And You will let us live again in Jerusalem." (Point to city walls, illustration #10.)

Nehemiah realized that a man would be needed to rebuild Jerusalem. Soon he understood that God had chosen him for that work. Do you think Nehemiah could simply pack up and go to Jerusalem? No, indeed! Remember, he had an important position. He would have to get permission from the king. This would not be easy for the king depended upon Nehemiah.

Once again Nehemiah prayed. "O God, please give me success. May I have favor in the presence of the king. Help me to know when and how to make my request."

Nehemiah prayed for four months. During all that time he served the king faithfully. He tried to look cheerful. To be sad in the king's presence could mean death! He tried to hide the sorrow in his heart. But it became harder and harder to do so.

3. NEHEMIAH'S PLAN
Nehemiah 2:1-10

One day Nehemiah was in the palace with King Artaxerxes. As usual, Nehemiah tasted the wine and handed it to the king.

Show Illustration #11

The king looked into Nehemiah's face. "Why are you sad?" he demanded.

Nehemiah was terrified. *Is the king angry with me?* he wondered. *Will the king get rid of me?*

To Artaxerxes, Nehemiah said, "Long live the king! Why should I not be sad? The city of my ancestors is buried in ruins. The gates have been burned down."

"What is your request?" asked the king.

Quickly Nehemiah silently prayed to the Lord. Then he answered the king. "Your majesty, will you please look favorably on your servant? Will you send me to Jerusalem to rebuild my fathers' city?"

Do you know what? The king immediately granted Nehemiah's request. He did. He really, truly did! King Artaxerxes wanted to know, however, when Nehemiah would return.

Nehemiah told him and added another request. "O king, would you please give me some letters? Will you write to the governors west of the Euphrates River? Please ask them if I may travel through their lands."

King Artaxerxes readily agreed.

Nehemiah had one more request. "O king, may I please have another letter? This one should go to Asaph, the keeper of your forest. I shall need wood to repair the city gates. And I shall need enough to build myself a house."

Again the king agreed. Think of it. The king gave Nehemiah everything he requested! He did so, Nehemiah said, because "the good hand of my God was upon me." The sovereign God had chosen Nehemiah for a special task. Therefore He prepared the way for His servant. The Lord caused the heathen king to be kind to Nehemiah.

King Artaxerxes did more than simply grant Nehemiah's requests. He also sent along a military escort to protect him. Twelve years before, this same king gave Ezra permission to travel to Jerusalem.

Had he sent troops to protect Ezra? (*No.*) Why not? (Review Lesson #2. Quote Ezra 8:22b. Emphasize that God does not deal with everyone the same way. He gives to each individual various opportunities, different training, varied problems. He is sovereign. He can work however He chooses.)

4. NEHEMIAH'S CHALLENGE

Nehemiah 2:11-3:32

When Nehemiah finally arrived at Jerusalem, he moved in quietly. He did not tell the Jewish leaders why he had come. He wanted to survey the amount of work to be done. He knew he would need the teamwork of many people.

One night after everyone was asleep, the city was perfectly quiet. Then Nehemiah and a few men silently checked the walls and gates.

Show Illustration #12

"Things are worse than I thought!" Nehemiah whispered. "Look at all this trash. We can hardly get though it!"

The next day Nehemiah gathered the Jewish leaders together. "Our city is a disgrace," he began. "It is in ruins. It is in danger because the walls are broken down. Anyone could attack us at any time. All the gates are burned. The situation is dreadful."

The leaders agreed. But they had no solution.

Nehemiah continued, "Many months ago Hanani told me about our ruined city. Since then I wept and prayed for Jerusalem. God chose me to come here to lead the rebuilding program. The Lord caused King Artaxerxes to let me come. And the king provided the materials we need. Men, let us rebuild the walls! Jerusalem must be an honor to the living God!"

The Jews responded, "Yes! Let us arise and build right now!"

God had prepared Nehemiah and sent him for this great task. Too, the Lord caused the Jewish leaders to accept Nehemiah's challenge.

"We shall rebuild these walls," Nehemiah told the leaders. "The God of Heaven will help us! We are His servants!"

Do you think the men succeeded in erecting the walls? We shall learn about this in our next lesson.

(*Teacher:* Display poster.)

Our lesson today included several instances of the sovereignty of God. Let us list these in our notebooks.

1. God sovereignly placed Nehemiah in the palace. There he learned to be a leader.
2. God entrusted Nehemiah with an important position with the king.
3. God burdened Nehemiah to rebuild Jerusalem.
4. God caused heathen King Artaxerxes to be favorable to Nehemiah's request.
5. God gave the Jews in Jerusalem enthusiasm for Nehemiah's challenge.

You are here today because God placed you here. As with Nehemiah, the Lord has a purpose for your life. He wants you to be His servant. How can you serve the living God of Heaven?

1. First, you must accept the Lord Jesus Christ as your Saviour.
2. You can serve God by obeying those in authority over you. (Children, Ephesians 6:1; Servants, Ephesians 6:5-8; Husbands and wives, Ephesians 5:22-30.)
3. You can serve the Lord by studying His Word heartily (Colossians 3:23-24).
4. You can serve the Lord God by being kind to others (Galatians 5:14).
5. You can serve God by telling others how to be saved (Philippians 2: 16a).

Nehemiah saw–and accepted–the opportunities God had for him. Will *you* pray for openings to serve the Lord this week?

Scripture to be studied: Nehemiah 3:1-10:39; Malachi 1:1-3:17

The *aim* of the lesson: To show that the sovereign God enables faithful people to do His work.

> **What your students should *know*:** That Satan continually tries to hinder God's sovereign work.
>
> **What your students should *feel*:** Confident that–despite problems–God can accomplish His sovereign plan in each life.
>
> **What your students should *do*:** Promise to obey the sovereign One and serve Him faithfully.

Lesson outline (for the teacher's and students' notebooks):

1. Nehemiah's strategy (Nehemiah 3:1-32).
2. Enemies' opposition (Nehemiah 4:1-23; 6:1-14).
3. Walls completed (Nehemiah 6:15-7:1).
4. Ezra's reforms (Nehemiah 7:2-4; 8:1-18; 9:26-28; 10:29-39; Malachi 1:1-3:17).

The verse to be memorized:

The hand of our God is upon all them for good that seek Him; but His power and His wrath is against all them that forsake Him. (Ezra 8:22b)

NOTE TO THE TEACHER

God has a plan for His people. And God accomplishes His plan. He chooses people to do His work. Sometimes people fail. Sometimes they sin. Nevertheless God in His sovereign time completes what He has planned. God's great enemy is Satan. Satan always tries to hinder God's work. But God is greater and at the end Satan is defeated.

Begin today's lesson by displaying poster: GOD IS SOVEREIGN. Review previous lessons carefully. Highlight God's sovereignty.

THE LESSON

Have others ever made fun of You? Did you like that? What did you do that caused them to laugh at you? What did you do when they mocked you? Did you ever make fun of someone else? Is that something we should do? Why?

Long ago Nehemiah and the Jews were laughed at. Some told lies about Nehemiah. To know how he reacted, listen carefully.

1. NEHEMIAH'S STRATEGY
Nehemiah 3:1-32

(*Teacher:* Review Lesson 3. Emphasize: (1) Nehemiah's challenge to rebuild the city walls, and (2) The enthusiastic response of the people.)

Nehemiah was a good leader. Where had he been trained? (*In the king's palace in Persia*) He knew how to get people to work. So first, he organized work teams. Each family belonged to one team. And each team worked on a section of the wall nearest their house. Before they could build the walls, they had to clean up the trash. Then they laid stone for the wall.

Show Illustration #13

Both men and women worked together. Merchants, priests, the city's leaders, craftsmen–everyone worked.

One leader talked as fast as he worked. "I thank the Lord for sending Nehemiah to help us. We should have done this long ago. We needed someone to challenge and lead us."

"You're right," a priest said. "We were in real danger with the walls broken down. Enemies could have attacked us at any time."

Another shouted, "Praise the Lord! Jerusalem will soon be beautiful and safe again!"

2. ENEMIES' OPPOSITION
Nehemiah 4:1-23; 6:1-14

But not everyone around Jerusalem was praising the Lord. Remember those who were angry when Zerubbabel began rebuilding the temple? (Review Lesson 1, section 3.) They–the Samaritan leaders–were dead now. But others had taken their places. Sanballat was one of them.

When Sanballat saw the walls being rebuilt, he was furious. He gathered some of his friends. "Do you see what those Jews are doing?" he asked. "Nehemiah has organized them into work teams. They're rebuilding the walls to fortify Jerusalem. Once the walls are built, the Jews will be strong. They may even try to rule us."

Show Illustration #14

Sanballat and his men went to the Jewish workmen. There they began to mock them. "What do you Jews think you are doing? Do you think you can build the walls in a day? Ha-ha! Look at those charred stones! Will you pull them out of the rubbish to use again? Ha-ha!"

Tobiah, another leader standing nearby, added to the ridicule. "If a fox (an animal like a small dog) walked on your wall, it would collapse! Ha-ha!"

Suppose you had been working on that wall. What would you have done? (Let students give suggestions: encourage honesty.) Would you have been tempted to throw rocks at them? Would you have shouted at them?

These Samaritans were trying to discourage the Jews. If the Jews became discouraged, they would not continue to work. So Nehemiah did as always when he had a problem. He prayed. Sh! Listen quietly and you will hear what Nehemiah prayed:

"Hear, O God; for we are despised: and turn their reproach upon their own heads, and give them for a prey in the land of captivity; and cover not their iniquity, and let not their sin be blotted out from before Thee: for they have provoked Thee to anger before the builders" (Nehemiah 4:4-5).

The Lord God heard and answered Nehemiah's prayer. The Jewish people continued to work hard and soon the wall was half finished (Nehemiah 4:6).

Sanballat and Tobiah had not been able to discourage the workers. So they–and other enemies of the Jews–had another scheme. They prepared to lead an army against Jerusalem. "Soldiers," Sanballat announced, "we shall make a surprise attack on the Jews! We shall confuse them and kill them. That will end their work."

Nehemiah heard about their enemies' plot. The Jews also heard about it. And they were discouraged and frightened.

Again Nehemiah talked to God about his problem. Then he spoke to his leaders and workers. "Do not be afraid," he said. "Remember the Lord. He is great and glorious. He will help us! From now on, half of you will stand guard. The others will work. Everyone must keep a weapon by his side. If enemies attack, fight for your families, your city, your home!"

Nehemiah continued, "On the wall we are separated from each other. So listen for the trumpet. When it sounds, stop what you are doing. Rush to the trumpeter. Remember, our God will fight for us!"

Nehemiah was a good leader. His wise plans encouraged the people. They returned to their task working from sunrise to sunset.

Sanballat learned that Nehemiah knew about the sneak attack. He gave up that idea, therefore, and worked on another.

This time Sanballat sent a letter to Nehemiah. "We would like to settle our differences with you," he wrote. "Come alone, Nehemiah, and meet with us. Let's talk things over."

Nehemiah realized this was a trick. By luring him away from Jerusalem they would try to kill him. He sent a message back saying, "I am doing a great work. Why should I stop to come meet with you?"

Sanballat did not give up. Four times he sent the same message. And four times Nehemiah sent the same reply.

"That Nehemiah makes me furious!" Sanballat exclaimed. Calling a servant he commanded, "Take this letter to Jerusalem. Read it publicly so all Jews will hear it."

When the servant reached Jerusalem he shouted, "Hear ye! Pay attention to the letter from Sanballat." People stopped their work and listened curiously. The servant read: "'I, Sanballat, understand you Jews are planning to rebel. For this reason you are building the city walls. And you, Nehemiah are planning to be king of the Jews. You are spreading the word that there is a king in Judah'." (See Nehemiah 6:4-8.)

Was this true? (*No*) Nehemiah knew it was a lie. So he wrote a letter to Sanballat. "You know that what you said is a lie. You know I have no plans to be king. And the people are not going to rebel. You are trying to scare us so we shall stop working. This we shall not do!"

Then Nehemiah prayed, "Dear Lord, please give me strength." After this, Nehemiah went on with his work. He left matters in God's hands.

Who was behind Sanballat's wicked plans? (*Satan*) Satan is God's enemy. He never wants God's work to prosper. So he causes wicked men to oppose God's people. This is true even today. But we have a wonderful promise. (Read to class 1 John 4:4.) Satan seemed to succeed for a while. But God defeated his schemes. The Lord God is sovereign. He is always in control of everything.

3. WALLS COMPLETED
Nehemiah 6:15-7:1

Show Illustration #15

"It is finished! It is finished!" the Jews shouted. "The wall is rebuilt! The gates are in place! Our city is safe!" Rejoicing and singing filled the air. What a happy day! People danced and clapped and embraced one another.

"Only 52 days and the work is done!" the people shouted. "No one could stop

us. The Lord God helped us. He is with us! God gave us a mind to work. And we worked together!"

The Lord had chosen and prepared Nehemiah to accomplish His work. God had given Nehemiah the wisdom he needed. He gave him strength for the task. Nehemiah was an excellent leader who willingly obeyed the Lord. Now he rejoiced to see God's work completed.

4. EZRA'S REFORMS
Nehemiah 7:2-4; 8:1-18; 9:26-28;
10:29-39; Malachi :1–3:17

The wall was finished. Nehemiah appointed his brother in charge of Jerusalem. Guards were assigned to watch the gates. Families were to guard the wall nearest their homes.

Several weeks later the people went to Ezra with a request. What do you remember about Ezra? (Read Ezra 7:10. Review highlights of Lesson 2, sections 2, 3, 4.) Ezra was still a leader in Jerusalem.

The people said, "Ezra, please read to us the law of God. We want to know what God instructed us through Moses." That was really a good request, wasn't it?

Show Illustration #16

The people listened carefully to the law of God. Sometimes they cried because they realized they had disobeyed Him. They rejoiced when they heard of God's faithfulness. Ezra reminded them that the Jews long ago had also disobeyed God. (See Nehemiah 9:26.) But when they repented, God forgave them. (See Nehemiah 9:28.)

"Our God is always ready to pardon," said Ezra. "He is gracious and merciful. He is slow to anger and full of love (Nehemiah 9:17). Our God keeps His promises (Nehemiah 9:8). Let us stand up and praise Him."

Then Ezra reminded them, "We are slaves here in our land. It is our own fault. God has punished us because of our disobedience to His laws. That is why King Artaxerxes is now our ruler. But today let us promise to follow the Lord God and serve Him."

"Amen!" shouted the Jews. "This is what we want to do."

So Ezra wrote an agreement and the people signed it. The agreement said:

1. We shall obey God's Law and observe all His commandments. (See Nehemiah 10:29.)
2. We shall not allow our children to marry the heathen people around us. (Nehemiah 10:30; see Deuteronomy 7:3-4.)
3. We shall not buy and sell on the Sabbath day. (Nehemiah 10:31; see Exodus 20:9-10.)
4. We shall pay the temple tax to meet the needs of temple worship. (Nehemiah 10:32; see Exodus 30:11-16.)
5. We shall bring regular offerings to be used in the house of God. (Nehemiah 10:33-39; see Exodus 23:19a; 13:2; Leviticus 23:17; Numbers 18:21, 26.)

God's Law required them to observe these matters. Now the Jews agreed to obey God, the holy, sovereign One.

The day arrived for the dedication of the new walls. It was a happy, thrilling day! Everyone brought offerings. The priests offered sacrifices. Singers came to Jerusalem from many villages. They sang heartily under the direction of the choirmaster. The choirs were accompanied by cymbals, harps, and trumpets.

The singing and rejoicing could be heard across the entire countryside. God gave the Jews great joy that day. It was a new beginning for them. They desired to serve their sovereign Lord– the One who is always in control of everything.

For a time the people kept their promises to God. But as the years passed, there were many changes.

Ezra died. Nehemiah died. The prophets **HAGGAI** and **ZECHARIAH** died.

The Jews forgot God. They ignored His commands. They began to marry the heathen people around them. They neglected God's temple. (See Malachi 1:13.) They did not even want to worship God!

Instead of bringing perfect sacrifices to God (as He had commanded), the priests offered diseased and crippled animals. (See Malachi 1:8, 13-14.)

The Lord was displeased with His people, the Jews (Malachi 1:10). They ignored Him. They disobeyed Him. And they were not sorry. God could have destroyed His people. But He still loved them (Malachi 1:2). So He sent another prophet, named **MALACHI**, to warn them of His punishment.

MALACHI spoke severely to the Jews, saying: "You are doing everything God hates. You marry the heathen. Then you divorce them. And God hates divorce." (See Malachi 2:16.)

MALACHI continued, "You wonder why your gardens dry up. Here is the reason: You are stealing from God. You do not bring your offerings to Him. You keep everything for yourselves. (See Malachi 3:8-11.) And God is punishing you."

The Israelites asked, "Why should we serve God? What will we get from serving Him?" (See Malachi 3:14.)

MALACHI, God's prophet, answered, "Come back to God's house! Return to studying His Word. Start doing His work." (See Malachi 2:7; 3:7, 10.) "If you turn to God, He will bless you greatly."

Some of the Jews listened to **MALACHI**. To one another, they said, "**MALACHI** is right. We have disobeyed the Lord. Let us turn to God, fear Him, and obey Him." (See Malachi 3:16.) Imagine that!

About 500 years after **MALACHI**, God gave His own dear Son, the Lord Jesus Christ for the sins of the world. All who truly trust in Him will be born into God's family and they will ever be with him in Heaven forever and ever. Will you be there? (*Teacher;* Explain clearly how to be born into the family of God.)

From these lessons we have learned that:

1. Our SOVEREIGN GOD moved the hearts of heathen kings. He used those kings to accomplish His plans for: (1) Rebuilding the temple; (2) Rebuilding the walls of Jerusalem.

2. God caused certain leaders (Zerubbabel, Ezra, Nehemiah) to return to Jerusalem to do His work.

3. God prompted some of the Jews to go with the leaders. Others gave money and supplies.

4. God gave the people a mind to work.

5. God defeated Satan's efforts to stop His work.

6. God never turned away from His people even when they disobeyed Him. He loved them. When they repented, He forgave them. He is the same to us today. (See 1 John 1:9.) We have the Bible to teach us how to obey and please God.

7. God is sovereign in our lives today. He placed us right where we are. He has given each one certain abilities. He gives us opportunities to use these abilities.

8. God is in control of all the world right now. He is accomplishing His plans for His whole universe.

9. Jesus Christ will come again to judge the wicked (all those who have turned away from Him). And when He comes, He will bless those who have turned to Him.

Will you (like Ezra and Nehemiah) choose to serve God? The Lord God can cause even the heathen to accomplish His purposes. But if you are His child, you may *choose* to be His servant. (***Teacher:*** For unsaved in your group, clearly explain the plan of salvation. See page 8.)

Ezra and the Jews made an agreement with God. Have you made an agreement with Him? Have you promised to read His Word daily and memorize Scripture? Have you agreed to pray? To obey those in authority over you? To be kind to others? To attend God's house?

Will you write your agreement this week and sign it? Place it in your Bible. Read it often. Ask God to help you keep it. Pray that you will be a useful servant of our sovereign Lord.

Made in the USA
Monee, IL
12 May 2022

96277540R00019